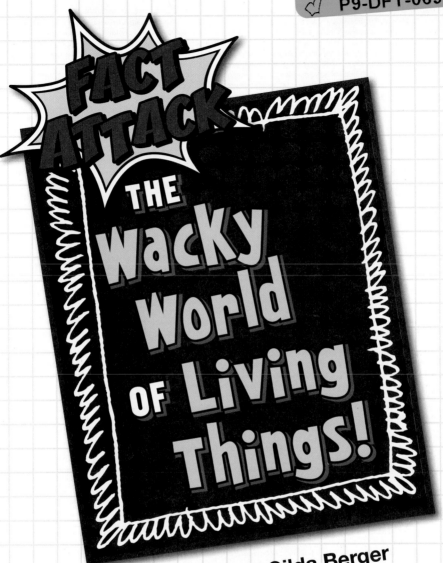

FACT ATTACK

THE Wacky World OF Living Things!

by Melvin and Gilda Berger

illustrations by Ed Miller

Scholastic Inc.

Photos ©: cover top: Pieter De Pauw/123RF; cover center: kikkerdirk/Thinkstock; cover bottom: AGioulis/iStockphoto; back cover: Ian 2010/Fotolia; 3: Chiyacat/Dreamstime; 4 top: Fabrice Beauchene/Fotolia; 4 bottom: Gale Verhague/Dreamstime; 5 top: Pavelmidi1968/Dreamstime; 5 bottom: jeanro/iStockphoto; 6-7: hometowncd/iStockphoto; 8-9: Syldavia/iStockphoto; 10 top: sasimoto/Fotolia; 10 bottom: 4FR/iStockphoto; 11 top: burnsboxco/iStockphoto; 11 bottom: Pniesen/Dreamstime; 12 left: USO/Thinkstock; 12 center: bearacreative/Thinkstock; 12 right: Craig Dingle/iStockphoto; 13 top: Unclesam/Fotolia; 13 bottom: Ecophoto/Dreamstime; 16: Michael Sheehan/Dreamstime; 18: iurii Konoval/iStockphoto; 19 left: Cathy Keifer/Dreamstime; 19 right: FedotovAnatoly/Thinkstock; 20 top: adogslifephoto/Thinkstock; 20 bottom: Sakdinon Kadchiangsaen/Dreamstime; 21: Mitja Mladkovic/iStockphoto; 26-27: elthar2007/iStockphoto; 28: Gleb_Ivanov/iStockphoto; 29 top: SBTheGreenMan/iStockphoto; 29 bottom: Marcel Auret/Dreamstime; 30 top left: Kavita/Fotolia; 30 top right: ksena32/Fotolia; 30 bottom: Bernhard Richter/Thinkstock; 31: Dimitris Kolyris/Dreamstime; 34 left: Oktay Ortakcioglu/iStockphoto; 34 center: showcake/Thinkstock; 34 right: Alexan2008/iStockphoto; 35 top: Roger Schaubs/Dreamstime; 35 bottom: skodonnell/iStockphoto; 36 top: Tina Rencelj/Dreamstime; 36 center left: ogurisu/Fotolia; 36 center right: MiaZeus/iStockphoto; 36 bottom left: mashuk/iStockphoto; 36 bottom right: c11yg/Fotolia; 37 top left: Richard Griffin/Fotolia; 37 top right: Chris6/Thinkstock; 37 center top left: Redwood8/Dreamstime; 37 center top right: Delpixart/Thinkstock; 37 center bottom left: ajt/Thinkstock; 37 center bottom center: gojak/iStockphoto; 37 center bottom right: marilyna/iStockphoto; 37 bottom left: Halil I. Inci/Dreamstime; 37 bottom right: Fabio Pagani/Dreamstime; 40-41: Cathy Keifer/iStockphoto; 44 top: Martingraf/Dreamstime; 44 bottom left: Rawpixelimages/Dreamstime; 44 bottom right: Kirill Kurashov/Dreamstime; 45 top: Kaan Ates/iStockphoto; 45 bottom: bajinda/Thinkstock; 48 top: Štěpán Kápl/Fotolia; 48 bottom: Alexander Shalamov/iStockphoto; 49 top left: popovaphoto/Thinkstock; 49 top right: Kenneth Schulze/iStockphoto; 49 bottom: FourOaks/Thinkstock; 50 top: Kmiragaya/Dreamstime; 50 center: Skye Hohmann/Alamy Images; 50 bottom: jeka1984/Thinkstock; 51 top: photofxs68/Thinkstock; 51 bottom: David Yang/iStockphoto; 54-55: ShaneGross/Thinkstock; 56 top: Jameson Weston/Thinkstock; 56 bottom: Michael Sheehan/Dreamstime; 57 top left: Billybruce2000/Thinkstock; 57 top right: iculizard/iStockphoto; 57 bottom: OlegIV/Thinkstock; 58 left: Kaan Ates/iStockphoto; 58 right: Clayton Hansen/iStockphoto; 59 top: GlobalP/Thinkstock; 59 center: Piccaya/Dreamstime; 59 bottom: pelooyen/iStockphoto; 60-61: Howard Chew/Thinkstock; 65: Andrew M/Dreamstime; 66: Zhykharievavlada/Dreamstime; 68 top: Mikael Males/Dreamstime; 68 center top: Jocrebbin/Dreamstime; 68 center bottom: Pius Lee/Dreamstime; 68 bottom: Zoran Kolundzija/iStockphoto; 69 top: Mario Madrona Barrera/Dreamstime; 69 center top: Gilitukha/iStockphoto; 69 center: Henkbentlage/Dreamstime; 69 center bottom: michael sheehan/Thinkstock; 69 bottom: Yaju Shrestha/Dreamstime; 70 left: vvvita/Thinkstock; 70 right: suerob/Fotolia; 71 top: reptiles4all/iStockphoto; 71 bottom: Kira Kaplinski/Dreamstime; 72 top: Cathy Keifer/iStockphoto; 72 bottom: eli_asenova/iStockphoto; 73: Claffra/Dreamstime; 74: Oleg Lopatkin/iStockphoto; 75 top: missty/Fotolia; 75 center: defun/Thinkstock; 75 bottom: Byelikova/Dreamstime; 78 top left: Ian 2010/Fotolia; 78 top right: Mordolff/iStockphoto; 78 center: Frank Leung/iStockphoto; 78 bottom: seksan44/iStockphoto; 79 left: Mikhail Blajenov/iStockphoto; 79 right: Sergey Kohl/Fotolia; 80 top: alenkadr/Thinkstock; 80 bottom left: MarcPo/iStockphoto; 80 bottom right: LUNAMARINA/Thinkstock; 81: USO/Thinkstock; 82 top: Cheryl Allison/Dreamstime; 82 center: Bluesunphoto/Dreamstime; 82 bottom left: Olga Khoroshunova/iStockphoto; 82 bottom right: Furtseff/Dreamstime; 83 top: ptaxa/iStockphoto; 83 bottom: Bhalchandra Pujari/Dreamstime; 84 top left: melvoys/Fotolia; 84 top center: jez_bennett/iStockphoto; 84 top right: Chrishowey/Dreamstime; 84 center left: Maurizio Bonora/iStockphoto; 84 center center: Janina Kubik/Dreamstime; 84 center right: highmountainphotography/Thinkstock; 84 bottom left: LUNAMARINA/Thinkstock; 84 bottom center: CoreyFord/iStockphoto; 84 bottom right: CoreyFord/iStockphoto; 85 top left: H_Yasui/Thinkstock; 85 top right: Steven Oehlenschlager/Dreamstime; 85 center left: Heather Patten/Dreamstime; 85 center right: StuPorts/Thinkstock; 85 bottom left: Andrea Zabiello/Dreamstime; 85 bottom right: FtLaudGirl/iStockphoto; 86-87: fotofritz16/Fotolia; 89: BIOphotos/iStockphoto; 90: Juliengrondin/Dreamstime; 91 top: Rufous52/iStockphoto; 91 bottom: Jerryway/Dreamstime; 94 left: Kmiragaya/Dreamstime; 94 right: Ian 2010/Fotolia; 95 left: defun/Thinkstock; 95 right: missty/Fotolia.

Copyright © 2017 by Melvin and Gilda Berger
Illustrations © 2017 Scholastic Inc.

Library of Congress Cataloging-in-Publication Data

Names: Berger, Melvin, author. | Berger, Gilda, author.
Title: The wacky world of living things! / by Melvin and Gilda Berger.
Description: First edition. | New York, New York : Scholastic Inc., 2017. |
Series: Fact attack | Audience: Ages 6-8. | Audience: K to grade 3.
Identifiers: LCCN 2016028660 | ISBN 9781338038392 (pbk.)
Subjects: LCSH: Animals—Miscellanea—Juvenile literature. |
Plants—Miscellanea—Juvenile literature. | Children's questions and answers.
Classification: LCC QH48 .B4645 2017 | DDC 031.02—dc23 LC record available at https://lccn.loc.gov/2016028660

10 9 8 7 6 5 4 3 2 1   17 18 19 20 21

Printed in the U.S.A.   40
First edition, July 2017

Book design by Ed Miller and Liz Frances
Photo research: Amla Sanghvi

Did you know that a **giraffe**'s tongue can reach its eyes?!

Ooh, do I have an itch!

Or that some **blueberries** are **pink**?

Inside **THIS BOOK** are 273 more **WACKY, CRAZY, GROSS, WILD, UNBELIEVABLE, SILLY, AWESOME** facts about animals and plants that will **AMAZE** you!

Turn the page and let your **FACTASTIC** adventure begin!

#1

A **narwhal whale** has the world's **LONGEST TOOTH:**

It can be up to **10** feet long!

#2

Female **emperor penguins** gather food for their families, while the males stand over the eggs.

#3

TASTY!

Butterflies taste with their feet.

#4

Crickets
have ears on
their knees.

knee

#5

An
**eagle's
nest**
can weigh
over two
tons.

#6 The **blue whale** is the most **HUMONGOUS** animal that has ever lived.

#9 It is **TALLER** than a four-story building.

flukes

#7 It is **HEAVIER** than **20** elephants.

dorsal fin

#8 It is **longer** than **three buses.**

flipper

#10 Its **SPOUT** can be the height of a **telephone pole.**

blowhole

#11 It has a **mouth** big enough to hold **100 kids.**

#12 It has a **HEART** the size of a small **car.**

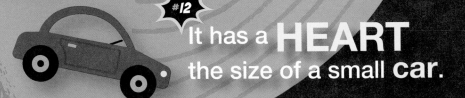

#13

Bulls are color-blind.

#14 They charge at bullfighters because they are waving their capes, NOT because the capes are red.

8

#15

COCONUTS
are giant seeds
that drop from
coconut trees.

#16

Hermit crabs
don't make their
own shells—they
simply move into
empty ones!

#17

A **crocodile** cannot stick out
its tongue.

#18

The hammerhead shark has both an eye and a nostril at each end of its head for hunting prey.

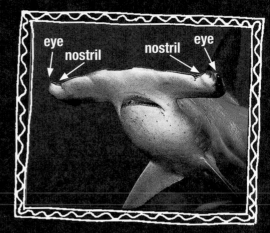

eye
nostril
nostril
eye

#19

Sea turtles have

flippers, not feet like land turtles.

flipper

flipper

#20

If a shark stops swimming, it will sink.

Now you tell me!

#21
An **elephant's toes**
are hidden *inside* its foot—so it is always walking on its

tiptoes!

#22
No birds living today have **teeth.**

#23

Some cactus plants have "wool" on the outside to protect them against frost and sun.

You smell good!

#24

Snakes smell with their tongues.

#25

The Brazilian railroad worm has a red light on its head and green lights along its sides.

Choo-Choo!

#26 Some animals can **grow new body parts** to replace those they lost in a fight or accident.

#27 A **starfish** can grow a new arm.

#29 A **crab** can grow a new claw.

#28 Some **lizards** can grow a new tail.

#30 A **tadpole** can grow a new tail.

#31

Some **worms** become two worms when cut in half—each with a head and tail.

#32

A **zebra fish** can grow a new fin.

#34

A **spider** can grow a new leg.

DOCTOR'S OFFICE

WAITING ROOM
Please take a seat

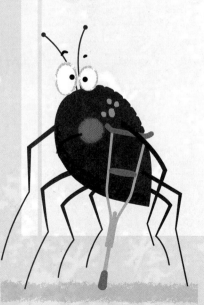

#33

A **conch** can grow a new eye.

#35 The **strongest bug**—the rhinoceros beetle—can lift an object 850 times its own weight.

#36 *A man with similar strength could lift 140,000 pounds!*

#37

Snakes don't have ears.

What?

#38

Only **female mosquitoes** bite.

#39 *They use the blood to make eggs inside their bodies.*

YUM!

#40

The **chow chow** dog is known for its black tongue.

#41 *Giraffes, polar bears, and a few other animals also have black tongues.*

#42

Squirting
cucumber
plants shoot their
seeds into the air.

#43

I saw that!

Chameleons can look in two
different directions
at the same time.

#44

The Stegosaurus,
one of the biggest dinosaurs,
had a brain the size of a walnut.

brain

#45

None for me, thanks. I had a big breakfast six months ago.

Most **snakes** can go a year without eating.

#46

Ants are a treat to eat in many parts of the world.

Yum! Yum! Yum!

#47

The **tongue** of an **anteater** looks like a rope.

#48

It is as long as a human arm.

#49 The **hoatzin** is the stinkiest bird in the world.

#50 *The bad smell comes from the rotting leaves it holds in its beak.*

#51 **Crocodiles** swallow stones to help them digest their food.

Meet some of the **smartest animals** on earth.

#52

Chimpanzees can be trained to communicate by computer keyboard or sign language.

#53

Orangutans make tools out of sticks to gather ants, eat fruit, and scratch their backs.

#54

Dolphins can learn to play ball, do tricks, and follow commands from humans.

#55

Parrots can learn hundreds of words, carry on conversations, and even count.

1, 2, 3, 4, 5,...

#56

Elephants remember distant water holes and recognize elephants they haven't seen for years.

#57

Pigs can learn to play video games and imitate each other.

#58

Crows work together to get food and to avoid enemies.

#59

Rats can be trained to shake hands, walk a tightrope, and jump through hoops.

Hello!

How do you do?

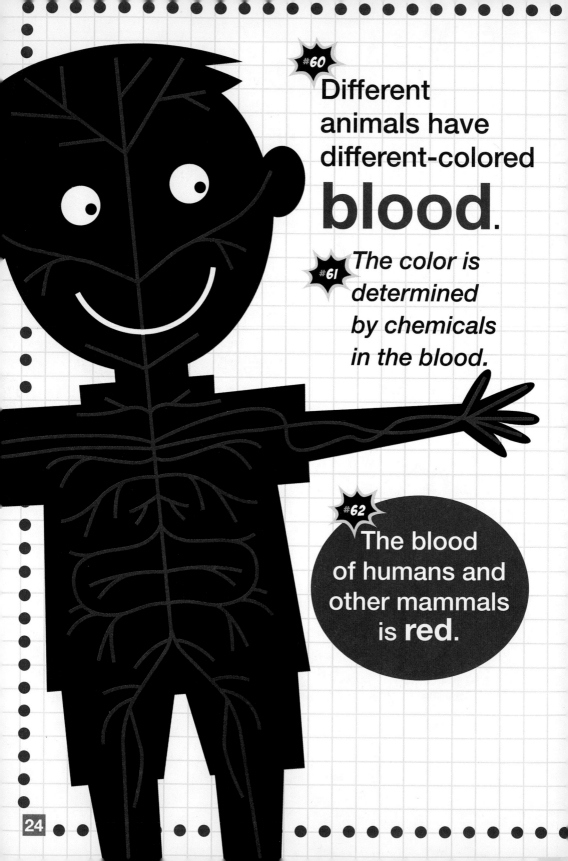

#60

Different animals have different-colored **blood.**

#61 *The color is determined by chemicals in the blood.*

#62 The blood of humans and other mammals is **red.**

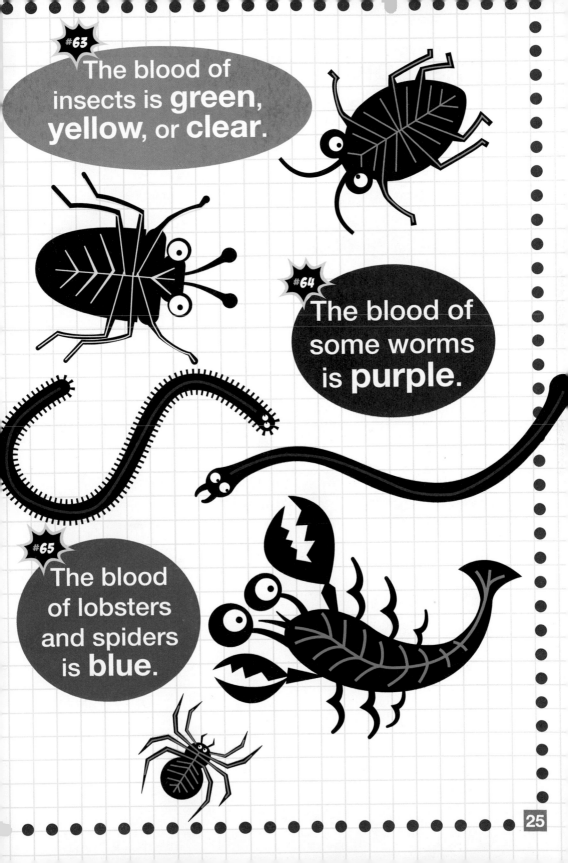

#63 The blood of insects is **green**, **yellow**, or **clear**.

#64 The blood of some worms is **purple**.

#65 The blood of lobsters and spiders is **blue**.

#66 **Most spiders have eight eyes.**
#67 *But some species of spiders have six, four, two—or even no eyes at all!*

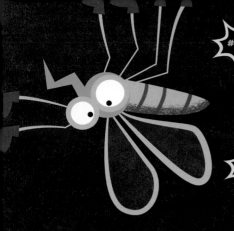

#68 FLIES can walk upside down on ceilings. **#69** *Tiny claws and sticky pads on their feet grip onto surfaces.*

#70 The **mandrill's** bright nose and behind help it find other mandrills in the dark jungle.

#71 A **rabbit's teeth** never stop growing. **#72** *Rabbits wear down their teeth by chewing—that way they never get too long.*

#73 Seeds of the **burdock plant** spread by hooking onto people's clothing and animal fur.

#74 **Polar bears** pick up smells seven times better than bloodhounds.

#75 **Crocodiles** can—and do—climb trees.

#76 *Adult crocodiles can climb as high as six feet off the ground, and the young can go even higher.*

#77

The **LEAVES** of a large oak tree give off 100 gallons of water by evaporation every day.

Aahh

#78

Worms

breathe through their skin.

#79

Monkeys burp to be friendly!

Hello!

BURP!

#80 The **homing pigeon** can always find its way home.

#81 *Iron in its beak and Earth's magnetism guide it in the right direction, like a compass.*

Pfff, I don't need a map!

ROAD MAP

#82 Scientists have grown a plant from a **32,000-year-old seed.**

#83 **Amazon ants** steal the young of other ants and force them to work as slaves.

#84 *The slave ants build homes and feed the Amazon ants—who only fight.*

#85 The NOISIEST animals in the world screech, scream, or roar louder than humans, whose average sound level is about 70 decibels. These animals' noises can be deafening!

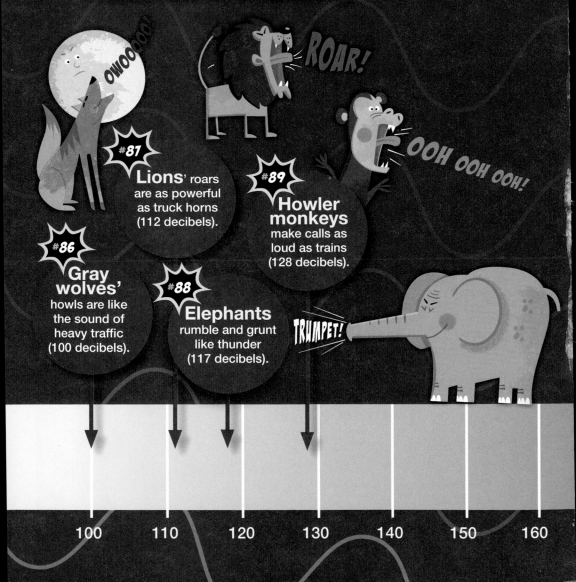

OWOOOOO!

ROAR!

OOH OOH OOH!

#87 Lions' roars are as powerful as truck horns (112 decibels).

#89 Howler monkeys make calls as loud as trains (128 decibels).

#86 Gray wolves' howls are like the sound of heavy traffic (100 decibels).

#88 Elephants rumble and grunt like thunder (117 decibels).

TRUMPET!

100   110   120   130   140   150   160

CLICK!
CLICK!
CLICK!

POP!
POP!
POP!

#90
Pistol shrimp form bubbles that burst like gunshots (200 decibels).

#91
Sperm whales click louder than jet planes at takeoff (230 decibels).

170   180   190   200   210   220   230

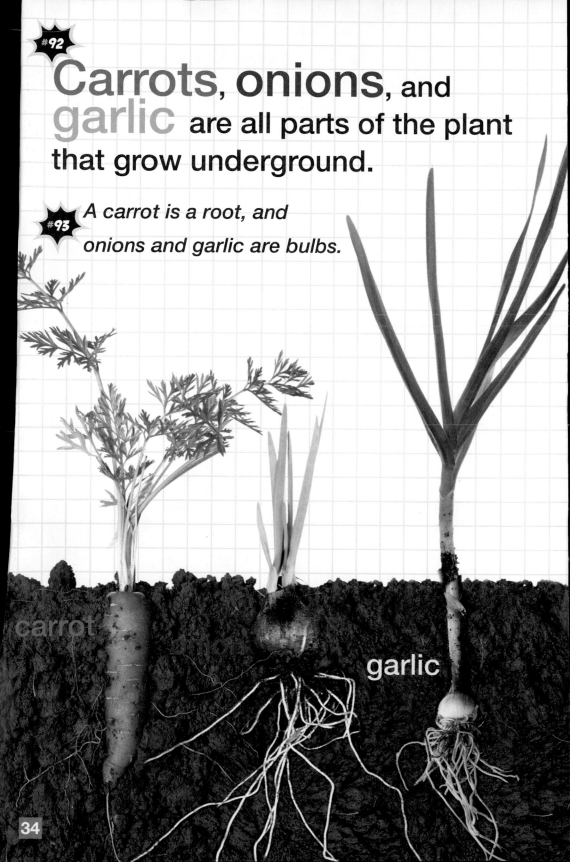

#92

Carrots, onions, and garlic are all parts of the plant that grow underground.

#93

A carrot is a root, and onions and garlic are bulbs.

carrot

garlic

#94

The seed of the

coco-de-mer palm tree

is the biggest seed in the world—twice the size of a basketball and about as heavy as an eight-year-old.

#95 *Orchids have the smallest seeds— five million of them weigh only about half an ounce.*

#96

Some plants are POISONOUS.
People who eat leaves, flowers,
fruits, seeds, or roots from these
plants can get sick and even die!

#97

Beware of ALL PARTS
of azaleas, dumb cane,
and laurel.

dumb
cane

azaleas

laurel

#98

Watch out for the LEAVES of
lily-of-the-valley and oleander.

oleander

lily-of-the-valley

#99

Stay away from the *BULBS* of daffodils, hyacinths, and narcissus.

daffodils

narcissus

hyacinths

#100

Don't be fooled by the *BERRIES* of mistletoe, holly, and yew.

mistletoe

holly

yew

#101

Steer clear of the *SEEDS* of castor beans and wisteria.

castor

wisteria

The number of **TEETH** in a shark's mouth is amazing!

#102

A shark has as many as **3,000** teeth.

#103

The teeth are lined up in **rows**, one behind the other.

#104

The **great white shark** has about 50 teeth in the front row alone.

 #105

When a shark **bites**, its front teeth often break or fall out.

 #106

Some sharks lose or break a tooth **every week**.

 #107

Each time a shark loses a tooth, another one **moves up** to take its place.

 #108

A shark can go through as many as 50,000 teeth in a lifetime!

#109

The **whale shark** has the most teeth of all—about 300 rows' worth!

#110

The **chameleon's tongue** is longer than its body.

#111

Many groups of animals

build homes, find food, keep safe, or raise young together— just like a family. A group of:

#112

bears is a sloth

#113

kangaroos is a troop

#114

chickens is a flock

#115

larks is an exaltation

#117

gorillas is a band

#116

frogs is an army

#118

hippos is a bloat

#119

crows is a murder

#120

foxes is a skulk

#121

cats is a clowder

#122

jellyfish is a smack

#123
buffalo is a **gang**

#127
lions is a **pride**

#128
rabbits is a **colony**

#129
hummingbirds is a **charm**

#124
toads is a **knot**

#125
sea otters is a **raft**

#130
owls is a **parliament**

LAW

#126
clams is a **bed**

Zzz...
Zzz...
Zzz...

#131
cattle is a **drove**

#132
whales is a **pod**

#133
geese is a **gaggle**

#134

Penguins
swim but cannot fly.

#135

NO plant naturally grows BLACK flowers.

#136

Rice is a plant that grows in flooded fields.

#137 *People eat rice with a fork in the United States, with chopsticks in China, or with their fingers in India.*

#138

The avocado has the most calories (234) of any fruit, and the cucumber, the fewest (16).

#139

Ants can swim.

#140

The **biggest horse** is about seven feet tall, which is taller than most basketball players.

#141

The smallest horse is only 17 inches tall—that's about the length of a newborn baby.

There are **20** billion **chickens** on Earth but only 7 billion people.

#143

Giraffes have only seven bones in their necks—the same number as humans.

1
2
3
4
5
6
7

#144

A **zebra** has stripes on its fur coat, but not on its black skin.

#145

To swallow, a **frog** pushes its eyes down on the top of its mouth, squeezing the food into its throat.

GULP!

#146

The **leaves** of the compass plant face north and south.

brain

#147

An **ostrich's eye** is bigger than its brain.

#148

Ants lived at the same time as the dinosaurs—more than 100 million years ago.

Hi, little friends!

#149

A **starfish** has no brain.

Huh?

#150

The world's slowest-growing tree is a species of **white cedar**, which takes 150 years to grow four inches.

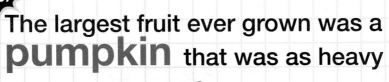

#151

The largest fruit ever grown was a **pumpkin** that was as heavy as a car.

Beep Beep!

#152 **Squirrels** rarely find all the nuts they bury in the fall. **#153** *Sometimes other squirrels find them first, and other times the nuts sprout into trees.*

#154

Hummingbirds

are the only birds that can fly forward, backward, upside down, and can hover in the air.

#155

A **polar bear** can smell a seal—its favorite prey—from 20 miles away.

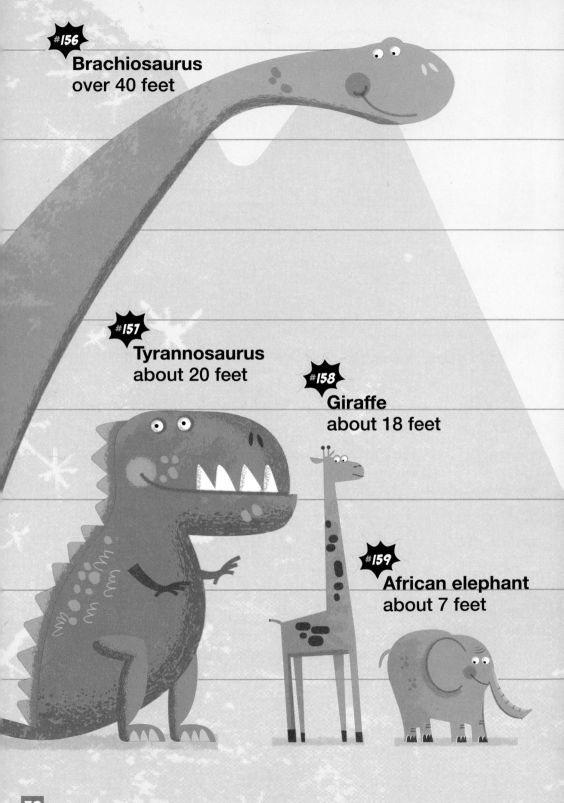

#156
Brachiosaurus
over 40 feet

#157
Tyrannosaurus
about 20 feet

#158
Giraffe
about 18 feet

#159
African elephant
about 7 feet

Animals come in many shapes and sizes, but a few stand out as the tallest animals that ever lived.

40 ft.

35 ft.

30 ft.

25 ft.

20 ft.

15 ft.

10 ft.

5 ft.

#160
Camel
about 6.5 feet

#161
Moose
about 6 feet

#162
Rhinoceros
about 5 feet

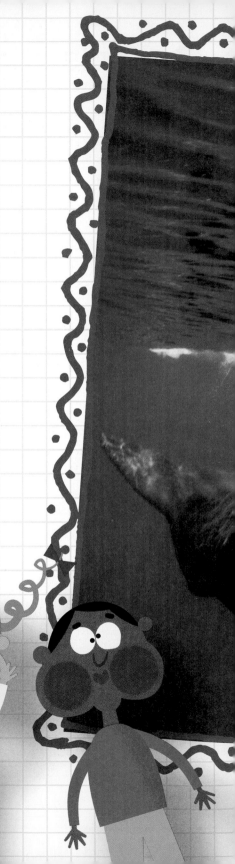

Sperm whales

can hold their breath underwater for over an hour!

#164 *Most people can't hold their breath longer than two minutes.*

#165

A cockroach
can live
nine
days
without
its head.

#166

A giraffe
gives birth while
standing—and
its calf drops
about six feet
to the ground.

#167

DUNG BEETLES
roll animal
poop into
balls—and
eat them.

#168

Ligers are the largest cats in the world.

#169 *They have lion fathers and tiger mothers, so they are never found in the wild.*

DAD LION   MOM TIGER

BABY LIGER

#170

Peanuts can be used as a main ingredient in dynamite.

#171 *The oil in peanuts is changed into nitroglycerin—an explosive.*

#172

Plover birds stand inside crocodiles' mouths to clean their teeth—without getting eaten!

You need to floss more!

Mayflies are born, lay eggs, and usually die within a day.

Monkeys grab and hold branches with the thumbs on their hands and feet.

The feet of a **gecko** have hairy pads that let it walk on walls and ceilings.

Scallops have tiny blue eyes along the edges of their shells.

People eat **fruits** and **vegetables** to stay healthy. But approximately how much produce does an average person eat in a year?

#177
28 pounds of corn

#179
29 pounds of carrots

#180
75 pounds of potatoes

#178
39 pounds of tomatoes

#181
44 pounds of onions

#182
32 pounds
of apples

#183
46 pounds
of bananas

#185
69 pounds
of lettuce

#184
25 pounds of
green beans

#186

All animals need to sleep, but some animals spend more than half the day sleeping!

HOURS OF SLEEP PER DAY

10 ——————

#187

Pigs and **pandas** sleep about 10 to 12 hours a day.

12 ——————

#188

Cats, hamsters, and **squirrels** sleep about 14 to 16 hours a day.

14 ——————

16 ——————

#189

Armadillos, opossums, hippos, and **lions** sleep about 17 hours a day.

18 ——————

#190

Koalas, sloths, and **brown bats** sleep about 18 to 22 hours a day.

20 ——————

22 ——————

#191

Some **bamboo** grows fast enough for the eye to see— about one and a half inches an hour!

#192

A female **codfish** can lay up to nine million eggs at a time.

#193

Snakes never close their eyes.

Zzz...

#194

The
GIANT SQUID
has the largest eyes of
any animal—about the
size of dinner plates.

#195 The most useful nose in the world is **six feet long** and belongs to the **elephant.**

The elephant uses its trunk to:

#196 **breathe** and **smell**.

#197 bring **food** and **water** to the elephant's mouth.

#198 **grasp** an object as small as a peanut.

#199 **lift** and **carry** up to a **ton** of logs.

#200 hold about one and a half gallons of water.

#201 give itself a shower.

#202 embrace its mate or young.

#203 wrestle other elephants.

#204 roar, rumble, grunt, and scream.

#205

The **swift** spends its whole life flying, only landing to lay eggs and care for its young.

Seriously? I have to keep flying?

PURR

MEW

MEOW

EOW

#206

Cats make more than 100 different sounds.

#207

Humans have kept **dogs** as pets for about **40,000 years.**

#208 The **horned toad** squirts blood from its eyes when threatened.

#209 The **Rafflesia** is the largest flower in the world.

#210 It is wider than a doorway and smells like rotting meat, which attracts insects.

Mmm, what is that delicious scent?

#211

A **tarantula**—the world's largest spider—can kill a bird, mouse, or other small animal with a blow from its front legs.

#212

The **honeybee** has about three million hairs—that's about as many as a squirrel!

#213

Some **snakes** are born with two heads.

#214 A two-headed snake named "We" lived in St. Louis's World Aquarium for eight years.

BURP!

#215

Only four mammals—elephants, hippos, rhinos, and sloths—cannot jump!

#216

Only half of all kinds of spiders spin webs to catch prey.

#217 *The ones that don't spin webs simply pounce on their prey, poison them, and eat them.*

#218
A **camel's hump** is filled with fat, not water.

#219 *This gives the camel energy, even when it doesn't have enough to eat.*

#220

Strawberries
are the only fruit with seeds on the outside.

#221

Termites can build 20-foot-tall nests, and each nest has room for one million termites.

#222

A person afraid of snakes is an **ophidiophobiac** (oh-fid-ee-oh-FOE-bee-ak).

#223 The average person in the United States lives to be almost **80 years old**, but the longest-living animals can grow to be even older!

#224 Eels can live more than 100 years.

#225 Galápagos tortoises can live about 190 years.

Happy birthday, kiddo!

#226

Greenland sharks can live about 300 years.

#227

Bowhead whales can live up to 210 years.

#228

Ocean quahogs can live more than 400 years.

#229 A **sunflower** is made up of hundreds of tiny flowers.

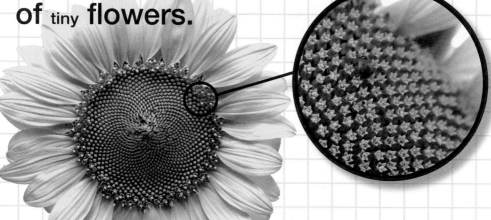

#230 **Pandas** eat only bamboo.

Bamboo again?

Always.

Take that!

#231 The **bombardier beetle** shoots boiling-hot poison at its enemies.

The **emperor tamarin** monkey was named for its big white **mustache**. Its mustache made it look like the German emperor Wilhelm II.

EMPEROR
TAMARIN MONKEY

EMPEROR
WILHELM II

EMPEROR (WILHELM?)
TAMARIN MONKEY

#233

Peanuts are beans, not nuts.

#234

The world's **tallest** tree— the California redwood—is taller than the Statue of Liberty.

#235 Spider **silk** is stronger than steel.

#236 A chimpanzee seems to smile when it is getting ready to attack.

#237 Mountain goats can walk up walls.

#238

Rhinoceros

horns are made of keratin, which is also found in human hair and fingernails.

Anyone got a nail file?

#239

The **albatross** is a giant bird that can glide for months on ocean winds without landing.

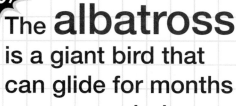

#240

A **polar bear** has black skin but looks white because of its translucent fur.

#241

Penguins
pant like dogs to cool off.

#242

Snakes
swallow their prey whole.

Did we fall in that hole again?

Let me out!

Hey, who turned the lights out?

#243

Whales have belly buttons.

belly button

The **fastest humans** can go only about 23 miles per hour, while the world's fastest animal moves around 200 miles per hour! Here are some of the maximum speeds:

In the Air

#245 Red-breasted merganser

#246 Spur-winged goose

#247 Frigate bird

Miles Per Hour (Average)   80   88   95

On Land

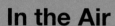

#250 Rabbit

#251 Ostrich

#252 Elk

Miles Per Hour (Average)   35   40   45

In the Sea

#255 Bluefin tuna

#256 Yellowfin tuna

#257 Marlin

Miles Per Hour (Average)   43   50

#248

White-throated
Needletail

#249

Peregrine falcon

106   200

#253

Pronghorn
antelope

#254

Cheetah

FINISH

60   65

#258

Swordfish

#259

Sailfish

60   68

#260

The **thorny devil** eats a meal
of 300 ants, one at a time.

Some plants trap and eat animals!

Venus flytraps

catch small animals
between their
snap-trap leaves.

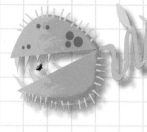

Corkscrew plants trap

insects between their twisted,
underwater leaves.

Bladderwort plants

suck small creatures into
underwater bags that spring
open and then slam shut.

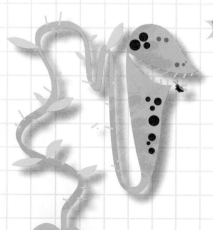

Pitcher plants

feed on insects
that fall into their
funnel-shaped
leaves.

Sundew plants nab insect prey with their sticky leaves.

The **wood** of an average tree can make **170,000** pencils.

#268 Mudskippers are fish that can climb trees.

#269 Tomatoes, pumpkins, cucumbers, and **eggplants** are actually fruits, not vegetables.

#270 Most fruits have seeds inside.

mwah!

#271 Lovebirds got their name because they look like they are kissing when they clean each other.

#272 There are more **insects** on Earth than any other kind of animal—about 10 quintillion of them!

#273 *Ten quintillion is a 10 followed by 18 zeros.*

Index